The Promises of God

A 31 Day Intensive Faith Therapy Devotional

By
Vanessa Collins

With Introduction by
Arlene Bell

Heart Thoughts Publishing
Floyds Knobs, IN

HEART THOUGHTS PUBLISHING

The Promises of God
Copyright © 2012 by Vanessa Collins

Request for information should be addressed to:
Heart Thoughts Publishing, P.O. Box 536, Floyds Knobs, IN 47119

ISBN-13: 978-0-9823325-3-5
ISBN-10: 0-9823325-3-x
LCCN: 2012938523

Unless otherwise indicated, the Scriptures quoted are taken from the Authorized King James Version of the Bible. Other translations used – The New Living Translation (NLT).

Cover Design: Vanessa Collins
Editor: Janice McCauly

Printed in the United States of America

First Printing, 2012

Dedication

To God, my Father: thank you for your promises.

To my wonderful husband Derrick and our wonderful children, Stephanie, Derrick II, David, and Tyrone and to my mom, Jean Crosby: thank you, again, for all that you do.

This book is especially dedicated to the 7 AM conference call family (Darla Adams, Arlene Bell, Andrea Blanton, Jean Blanton, Gloria Boyton, Daryl Bramlett, Juliet Bramlett, Derrick Collins, Keisha Collins, Kevin Collins, Jean Crosby, Tammie Curry, Diane Elias, Rita Haywood, Cindy Lee, Carestella McGhee-Abrams, Cindy McGhee-Junkins, Sandra Mitchell, Almeda Nelson, Betty Parnell, LaShonne Randolph, Mary Ray, Georgia Sanders, Paul Southerland, and Yvonne Wallace). Words cannot describe how much you have helped me over the last few years. Without you, this project would not have been conceived.

Table of Contents

Introduction

GOD....the One who stepped out in total darkness, uttering words that created a world which had been without shape and void. God said, "Let there be" and "it was", and shall ever be. Part of His plan at creation was to prepare a place for His most prized creation to dwell and have dominion over. Our God was planning, preparing and thinking of you and me. He has made promises to us that will show us His unfailing love. Promises made are promises kept.

God, the creator, knows our name, our situations and has given each of us a road map to a life of prosperity, health and faultless presentation to Him at the last day. Know and enjoy this 31 day meditation plan. Be blessed by it and thank God for the writer, Rev. Vanessa L. Collins.

Arlene Bell

Day 1- The Lord That Heals You

Scripture Lesson: Exodus 15:26

> *And said, If thou wilt diligently hearken to the voice of the LORD thy God, and wilt do that which is right in his sight, and wilt give ear to his commandments, and keep all his statutes, I will put none of these diseases upon thee, which I have brought upon the Egyptians: for I am the LORD that healeth thee.*

Meditation
It was a tremendous time for the children of Israel. They had just witnessed what had to be the biggest miracle any of them had ever seen. The Red Sea miraculously opened for them as they were being chased by Pharaoh and his army. It had to be tremendous to see the floating bodies of men, horses and chariots in a sea that they just passed over on dry land. What a time of praise! And they did just that. Miriam, Moses and the rest of the children of Israel gave God tremendous praise. That is, until the next problem surfaced.

It had been 3 days since they had water. They were getting thirsty. The songs stopped. The timbrels were quiet and the murmuring began. They did find water but it was bitter and could not be consumed. "What are we to drink?" they complained to Moses.

Moses could do nothing but cry. How disheartening! After such wonderful miracles, after God had shown Himself to be so strong and such a wonderful provider and protector, all they could do was murmur. None of the children of Israel said, "Let's pray and ask God for water" or "Let's pray and ask God for wisdom". Rather than looking at what God had already done, they chose to complain about the situation. Moses cried out to God. In response, God did for Moses what He has promised to do when we cry out to Him; He gave Moses wisdom. He showed Moses what to do and it made the waters drinkable.

It is from this teaching session that we get our promise for today. God promised them that if they would do right in His sight and obey His laws, He would not bring sickness on them as He had done the Egyptians because He is the God that heals them. Healing is in His nature. However, disobedience, along with their current attitude, would bring about sickness.

How does this promise affect us today? Unfortunately, the children of Israel did not walk in obedience, and as a result, they often found themselves under the curse of sickness. The healing promised here is conditional. Unfortunately, neither the children of Israel nor us today can keep our end of the promise. However, this promise is special in that it speaks to the nature of God which is independent of the nature of man. Since we could not walk in healing that resulted in obedience, The God that healeth us, Jehovah Rapha, had another way. He would include healing as part of the salvation package and take care of our physical healing with our spiritual healing. By the stripes of Jesus, we were healed. Therefore, our healing is not dependent on our obedience to the law. It is dependent on our ability to believe the Word of God concerning our healing. As Jesus often told those that sought Him for healing, "According to your faith be it unto you".

Affirmations
Healing is in God's nature. He has included healing in my salvation package. By the stripes of Jesus, I was healed. Therefore, healing is mine. I will cast down any thoughts of sickness and disease and meditate on thoughts of wellness, wholeness and health. I am so grateful for the fact that God is my Jehovah Rapha, the Lord that heals me. In Jesus' name, Amen.

Day 2 - I Will Take Sickness Away From You

Scripture Lesson: Exodus 23:25

And ye shall serve the LORD your God, and he shall bless thy bread, and thy water; and I will take sickness away from the midst of thee.

Meditation

The children of Israel have arrived at Mt. Sinai and they are receiving the laws of God. In Exodus chapter 20, God, through Moses, gives them what is known as the "Ten Commandants". The following chapters include other laws that they are to follow. These laws covered workers, personal injury, property damage, theft and a host of other things. The laws would provide a foundation for their government and social order for the children of Israel and establish them as a strong, orderly nation.

God also gave them instructions about the conquest they had to undertake. Although God had given them the "promised land", they would still have to take dominion of it. God did not drive out the occupants before they came, He would use the Israelites to drive them out. He would do it in an orderly manner so that the land would not lay barren and overtaken by animals. God had a plan. However, the Israelites would have to do their part in order for the plan to be successful.

God explains to them that He is sending the Angel of the Lord before them. The Angel of the Lord is known to be a pre-incarnate appearance of Jesus. God warns them not to provoke this Angel. He does not play. God tells them that He will not forgive them. But if they will obey the voice of this Angel and do what He says, they will be successful.

This brings us to our promise for today. God tells them that if they would just serve the Lord their God, He would not only bless their food and water, He would take sickness away from their midst. God had already introduced Himself to them as Jehovah Rapha, The Lord that heals in Exodus 15:26. We see again, it is God's nature to heal.

Consider God's character as revealed here. Not only will He heal them, He would take sickness away from their midst. Sickness would not even be in the air. They did not have to worry about catching something. They would live without the threat of contagious viruses or bacteria. He goes on further to say that there would be no miscarriages or barrenness, and everyone would live to the fullness of their days.

God's character does not change. He still desires to direct us in the dominion that He has assigned to us. He still wants us to live in health and wholeness with none barren. We do not have to walk in fear of every news report we hear about sickness and disease around us. He still wants us to live to the fullness of our days. It's His character, and He is the same yesterday, today and forever more.

Affirmations

God wants me to be successful in the "promised land" He has assigned for me. I will walk in the dominion that God has designated for me. I will listen to the voice of the Holy Spirit. I will serve the Lord. I know that by Jesus' stripes, I am already healed. I am so grateful for the promise that God will take sickness from around me. In Jesus' name, Amen.

Day 3 - I Will Restore Health to You

Scripture Lesson: Jeremiah 30:17
> *For I will restore health unto thee, and I will heal thee of thy wounds, saith the LORD; because they called thee an Outcast, saying, This is Zion, whom no man seeketh after.*

Meditation

Jeremiah spent over 40 years proclaiming a message of doom to the stiff-necked people of Judah. The stubbornness of his people, as well as the harshness of God's judgments, would often bring him to tears, earning him the name of the "weeping prophet".

Jeremiah did not accept his prophetic gift as readily as Isaiah did. Jeremiah complained that he was only a child and did not know how to speak, although he came from a priestly family. God insisted that Jeremiah go and proclaim His word. Jeremiah obeyed.

At this point, God was fed up with Judah. He had determined the disaster that would befall them. To make it worse, the people would not listen to Jeremiah's words and chose to believe false prophets that proclaimed that everything would be all right.

Jeremiah chapter 30 does not paint a comforting picture for Judah. God has proclaimed that their wounds would be grievous because of the multitude of their sin. However, He does give them a ray of hope. It is in this ray of hope that we find our promise for today.

Although God would bring this mighty judgment on Judah, He promises to restore their health and heal their wounds. This does not just speak to individual healing but healing as a nation. Even in God's immense anger toward this nation, He still speaks of healing them. This once again shows that healing is truly God's nature and character.

If you are dealing with a physical challenge, meditate on the fact that healing is in God's nature. He designed your body to heal itself under normal circumstances. However, when circumstances are not normal and you find yourself not walking in divine health, you can seek God. Healing is His nature. He is Jehovah Rapha, the Lords that heals. Walk in your healing today.

Affirmations

I find comfort in the fact that healing is in God's nature. I do not have to walk in sickness or disease. I can proclaim that by the stripes of Jesus, I was already healed. I am so grateful for the promise that God will restore health to me and heal my wounds physically, mentally and spiritually. In Jesus' name, Amen.

Day 4 - I Will Heal Their Land

Scripture Lesson: 2 Chronicles 7:14

If my people, which are called by my name, shall humble themselves, and pray, and seek my face, and turn from their wicked ways; then will I hear from heaven, and will forgive their sin, and will heal their land.

Meditation

King Solomon had completed the biggest project of his reign. He built the temple of God. What an honor! Although this was a dream of his father, David, God chose to give this project to Solomon. It was magnificent and would become one of the Seven Wonders of the Ancient World. This day, the day for the dedication of the temple, was for God. He made sure to try to show God his love and admiration. He sacrificed thousands of burnt offerings in an attempt to show God how much he cared. He prayed earnestly that God would be pleased with his efforts and that God would honor this place as His dwelling place.

Solomon also prayed about the sins of the people. Not their current sins, but their future sins. Being wise, Solomon knew how hard it was to walk according to the law. He struggled with it and knew his people did also. But He loved God and he wanted to be assured that their sins would not separate them too far from God. God responded to Solomon's prayer in an awesome way. First, He sent fire from heaven to consume the sacrifice. He then filled the temple with His glory so strongly that the priest could not enter in. Finally, He verbally responded to Solomon's prayer in dream a week later. It is from this response that we get our promise for today.

God explains the power that the people have concerning judgments that would come as a result of sin. He tells Solomon that if He decides to judge the people by drought, locust or sickness, that there is a way out. If His people, which are called by His name, would humble themselves, and pray, and seek His face, and turn from their wicked ways; then will He hear from heaven, forgive their sin, and heal their land. Again, we see Jehovah Rapha, The Lord that Heals, at work. Even in the face of sin, God is ready to heal. Healing is truly in God's nature.

Although this seems like a pretty easy formula to follow, the children of Israel were not able to do it on a consistent basis. As a result, they lost the land that God had promised to heal and are still, to this very day fighting for the promise land that God gave them.

For the New Testament Christian, this verse can be summed up in one word, JESUS. It is through Jesus that we humble ourselves before God. It is in the name of Jesus that we now pray. It is through Jesus that we seek the face of God since Jesus said if we see Him, we see the Father. It is through Jesus that we have access to the Holy Spirit, whereby we can trade our wicked ways, or works of the flesh, for the fruit of the Spirit. And finally, it is through Jesus that we realize the promise. God hears us from heaven, He forgives our sins and He heals our land.

Affirmations

God is my Jehovah Rapha, The Lord that Heals. I thank God for my salvation through Jesus Christ. I thank God for the abiding Holy Spirit. I rejoice and am grateful for the fact that God hears us from heaven, forgives our sins and heals our land. In Jesus' name, Amen.

Day 5 - I Will heal Him

Scripture Lesson: Isaiah 57:18-19

I have seen his ways, and will heal him: I will lead him also, and restore comforts unto him and to his mourners. I create the fruit of the lips; Peace, peace to him that is far off, and to him that is near, saith the LORD; and I will heal him.

Meditation
The prophet Isaiah prophesied to the Kingdom of Judah for over 40 years. The Book of Isaiah contains some of the most incredible prophecies in the Bible. Isaiah describes in detail the coming of the Messiah and the future reign of Jesus Christ. He warns both the Northern and Southern kingdoms of the severe punishment that God had declared because of their sins. However, just as Jeremiah, he tells of restoration and promise.

The Living Bible Translation states Isaiah 57:18-19 like this: *"I have seen what they do, but I will heal them anyway! I will lead them. I will comfort those who mourn, bringing words of praise to their lips. May they have abundant peace, both near and far,"* says the Lord, who heals them." God continues to declare himself as Jehovah Rapha, the Lord that Heals. Even though God knows what they do, He declares that He will heal them anyway. He has chosen them. They are His people.

God has chosen us. We have responded by accepting Jesus as our Lord and Savior. As our Lord and Savior, Jesus took our punishment and secured our salvation. Our salvation package includes accomplished healing. Not healing to come, but healing that has already been accomplished.

As we review the promises of God regarding healing, let's renew our mind to the fact that healing is in God's nature. God designed us by nature to be healed. Our bodies were designed with systems and hormones specifically designed to prevent sickness and to heal us if sickness occurs. The whole purpose of the immune system is to protect our bodies against infection. However, we are uninformed about how our bodies work. And even the information that we do know, we refuse to act upon. For instance, the majority of people will say that they know they don't drink enough water. Even with this knowledge, they will say that a week from now, a month from now, even a year from now. Although they have the information, the behavior has not changed. We must be better stewards of our bodies and learn how our bodies work. Once we learn, we must act on that information.

Affirmations
It is God's nature to heal. He is my Jehovah Rapha. I will never again question whether it is God's will to heal me. By the stripes of Jesus, I was already healed. I will walk in this revelation. I will listen to Holy Spirit and do those things needed to take care of my body. In Jesus' name, Amen.

Day 6 - I Will Strengthen You and I Will Help You

Scripture Lesson: Isaiah 41:10

> *Fear thou not; for I am with thee: be not dismayed; for I am thy God: I will strengthen thee; yea, I will help thee; yea, I will uphold thee with the right hand of my righteousness.*

Meditation

In order to deal with fear, we must understand it. There is a lot of information about fear. Psychologists and sociologists are constantly studying the effect of fear. We do not have to have a master's degree to understand the effects of fear. We have all experienced fear in our lives. Whether it was being chased by a dog, having to face your parents after you were caught doing wrong or hearing devastating news, fear can have a lasting effect on your life.

Fear can be paralyzing and not in just a figurative way. Fear is an emotional response to a perceived threat. The emotion of fear can produce thoughts in your mind which will send actual messages to your physical body. Your heart will start beating faster, your palms may get sweaty, and you definitely will feel something in your stomach. Fear can literally stop you in your tracks where your legs cannot physically move, even though they have not sustained any injury.

So how do we overcome our fears? There are tons of books, articles, workshops and seminars on this subject. However, to overcome fear, you must look at the root of fear. Fear is an emotion. An emotion is simply a monitor of our mental state. You cannot overcome fear by trying to reduce the emotional response. You must overcome fear by addressing the thoughts which are causing the response.

The thought which usually causes fear is helplessness. When an event happens, our minds process that event. The thoughts that we think, as a result of the event, will trigger the appropriate emotional response. If we feel helpless as a result of the event, fear will set in. Feelings that we express with words, such as "I don't know what I am going to do", "I don't know how to handle this", and "I can't solve this problem", speak to helplessness, which speaks to fear.

In this verse, God speaks to our helplessness. He promises to help us. He promises that He will be with us, He will strengthen us and He will hold us up. Let this sink in. The all-powerful God promises to help you. A real understanding of this will force the thoughts of helplessness out the door. Scripture tells us that God has not given us a spirit of fear, but of peace, love and a sound mind. The Psalmist reminds us that God is a very present help in the time of trouble. So, let's look at our problems with a sound, rational mind. If the Almighty God of the universe has promised to help us, what do we have to fear? What can overtake us?

Can God fulfill this promise? What if I need God and He is busy? God can fulfill this promise because God is never too busy. He will always get there in time, because He is already there. You have the power of God available to you at all times. Fear not, you are not helpless.

Affirmations

God has not given me a spirit of fear, but of peace, love and sound mind. I am not helpless. God has promised to be with me, strengthen me, and uphold me. I am so grateful for the promise that God will help me. In Jesus' name, Amen.

Day 7 - I Will Hold Your Right Hand and Help You

Scripture Lesson: Isaiah 41:13
For I the LORD thy God will hold thy right hand, saying unto thee, Fear *not; I will help thee.*

Meditation

We are continuing to look at the promises of God that encourages us not to fear. As we discussed previously, fear is an emotion that usually stems from thoughts of helplessness. We must examine the thoughts that are producing fear before we can deal with fear. Fear is really just a symptom which tells us that there is a perceived threat in our mind.

There is a definition of fear that has been floating around the Body of Christ for years. It defines fear as "False Evidence Appearing Real". Most of the things we fear have no real basis. And those that have real basis also have real solutions. As Franklin D. Roosevelt said, "We have nothing to fear but fear itself."

Our promise today paints the picture of a loving Father holding the hand of His scared child. In the previous verses, God tells His people that they should not fear because He will help them. He repeats this promise again. "Fear not, I will help you." Furthermore He tells them that He will hold their hand. What a loving Father!

Allow these words to penetrate your mind and spirit. "Fear not, I will help you." Whatever you are facing, hear these words, "Fear not, I will help you." If you are dealing with a physical challenge, hear your Father say, "Fear not, I help you." If you are dealing with a financial challenge, hear Him say, "Fear not, I will help you." If you are dealing with other obstacles or challenges, hear the Almighty God tell you, "Fear not, I will help you."

After you have meditated on these words, act on them. Allow God to help you by accepting His help. Yield to the leading of the Holy Spirit. Be on the lookout for solutions that you thought could not come. Look for the manifestations of things that you have believed God for. Trust Him and do not yield to fear.

Affirmations

God has not given me a spirit of fear, but of peace, love and a sound mind. I will accept God's help. I will yield to the leading of the Holy Spirit. Because my heavenly Father has promised to help me, I will not give in to fear. I so am grateful for the promise that God holds my hand and He helps me. In Jesus' name, Amen.

Day 8 - I Will Help You

Scripture Lesson: Isaiah 41:14
> *Fear not, thou worm Jacob, and ye men of Israel; I will help thee, saith the LORD, and thy redeemer, the Holy One of Israel.*

Meditation

We continue to look at the command from God to fear not. We have seen in the last 5 verses of scriptures, Isaiah 41:10-14, that God has told Israel to "fear not" 3 times. He gives them the same reason each time. They do not have to fear because He will help them. Although they have brought these conditions on themselves, their loving Father says that He will strengthen and uphold them. That's a powerful promise from a powerful God.

In our promise today, we see another aspect of God. God tells them that He is their redeemer. There are several definitions of redeemer in the dictionary and we can see God in all of them. A redeemer is one who:

- recovers ownership of by paying a specified sum
- pays off (a promissory note, for example)
- turns in (coupons, for example) and receives something in exchange
- fulfills (a pledge, for example)
- sets free; rescue or ransom
- saves from a state of sinfulness and its consequences
- makes up for
- restores the honor, worth, or reputation of

God assures them that He can help them because He is their redeemer. Thank God, He is our redeemer also.

Here's an interesting thing to consider. We have often heard that the fall of man in the garden sold us to Satan and that redemption was not available until the coming of Jesus. We are truly redeemed by the sacrifice of Jesus on the cross. But God establishes Himself as Israel's redeemer over 700 years before Jesus came. As their Father, He claims the position of redeemer for these people who needed Him right then. They did not need a redeemer that would not be on the scene for another 700 years. They needed help right then, and they received it.

The Bible tells us that God is a very present help in the time of trouble. As New Testament Christians, we have even better promises than those of the Old Testament saints. We have the Almighty Father, the Son Jesus, and the precious Holy Spirit all residing in us at the same time. What room should there be for fear? Our help is on board.

Affirmations

God is my refuge and my strength, a very present help in the time of trouble. I have been redeemed by the sacrifice of Jesus Christ. I choose not to fear. I am so grateful for the promise that God helps me. I am so excited to walk in courage and victory in every area of my life. In Jesus' name, Amen.

Day 9 - I Have Redeemed You

Scripture Lesson: Isaiah 43:1

But now thus saith the LORD that created thee, O Jacob, and he that formed thee, O Israel, Fear not: for I have redeemed thee, I have called thee by thy name; thou art mine.

Meditation

In our lesson today, God tells Israel not to fear because He has redeemed her. As we saw in the previous lesson, the word "redeemed" means to buy back or save from a state of sinfulness. God has staked His claim to Israel. He has called her by name and Israel is His. What a wonderful picture of a loving God and Father. Since God provided our redemption through the sacrifice of Jesus Christ, we too share in this promise.

The next verses establish why we can walk in victory. In the Living Bible Translation it reads:

> *"When you go through deep waters, I will be with you. When you go through rivers of difficulty, you will not drown. When you walk through the fire of oppression, you will not be burned up; the flames will not consume you."*

Although you may go through trials and tribulations, God promises to be there with you so that you can be successful in all that you go through. Notice, He does not say that He will be there to watch you get overtaken. He will be there so that you can be victorious. You will not drown, and you will not be consumed.

When challenging situations present themselves, focus on your help, not the challenge. Realize that you have a redeemer and your redeemer lives. God has promised to be there with you because He is already there. He is not there to watch you fall. He is there to strengthen you and uphold you. He has promised you victory in the face of challenging situations. Walk in your victory.

Affirmations

I have been called by name. I belong to God. I am redeemed. I do not have to walk in fear because God has told me to fear not. I am so grateful for the promise that God has redeemed me. In Jesus' name, Amen.

Day 10 - I Will Pour My Blessing

Scripture Lesson: Isaiah 44:2-3, 8

Thus saith the LORD that made thee, and formed thee from the womb, which will help thee; Fear not, O Jacob, my servant; and thou, Jesurun, whom I have chosen. For I will pour water upon him that is thirsty, and floods upon the dry ground: I will pour my spirit upon thy seed, and my blessing upon thine offspring:...Fear ye not, neither be afraid: have not I told thee from that time, and have declared it? ye are even my witnesses. Is there a God beside me? yea, there is no God; I know not any.

Meditation

We have seen in our previous lessons that God has told us not to fear because He is there to help us. He promises to strengthen us and uphold us. How can He do this? He is God and besides Him there is no other.

Isaiah chapter 44 is a great chapter to get a glimpse of the personality of God. God does not suffer from self-esteem issues. God does not doubt who He is. As His children, we should walk in this same confidence. Listen to the first 8 verses of this chapter as recorded in the Living Bible Translation.

> "But now, listen to me, Jacob my servant, Israel my chosen one. The Lord who made you and helps you says: Do not be afraid, O Jacob, my servant, O dear Israel,¹ my chosen one. For I will pour out water to quench your thirst and to irrigate your parched fields. And I will pour out my Spirit on your descendants, and my blessing on your children. They will thrive like watered grass, like willows on a riverbank. Some will proudly claim, 'I belong to the Lord.' Others will say, 'I am a descendant of Jacob.' Some will write the Lord's name on their hands and will take the name of Israel as their own." This is what the Lord says— Israel's King and Redeemer, the Lord of Heaven's Armies: "I am the First and the Last; there is no other God. Who is like me? Let him step forward and prove to you his power. Let him do as I have done since ancient times when I established a people and explained its future. Do not tremble; do not be afraid. Did I not proclaim my purposes for you long ago? You are my witnesses—is there any other God? No! There is no other Rock—not one!"

God knows who He is. Do you know who you are? You are His child. He made you. Therefore, He tells you that you do not have to be afraid. He will quench your thirst and water your dry fields. What happens when you add water to dry fields? They begin to produce. They thrive. God had promised that He will do His part in order for us to thrive. He is God, and besides Him there is no other.

Affirmations

There is no God besides our God. He is the beginning and the end. I will not walk in fear. I will walk in courage and victory. God has promised to help me and I believe that He is able to do what He promises. I am so grateful for the promise that God will pour His blessing upon me. In Jesus' name, Amen.

Day 11 - I Will Turn Their Mourning into Joy

Scripture Lesson: Jeremiah 31:13

Then shall the virgin rejoice in the dance, both young men and old together: for I will turn their mourning into joy, and will comfort them, and make them rejoice from their sorrow.

Meditation

Let's turn our attention to joy. Our lesson today is based on a teaching done by Derrick Collins at Redeeming Ministries several years ago.

In this lesson, Minister Collins used the following definition of joy: "positive attitude or pleasant emotion; delight." He explained that many kinds of joy are reported in the Bible. Even the wicked are said to have experienced joy in their triumphs over the righteous. Many levels of joy are also described including gladness, contentment, and cheerfulness. The joy that we have as children of God rises above circumstances and focuses on the very character of God.

In our lesson for today, we see God speaking through the prophet Jeremiah concerning the return of the children of Israel to their land. The nations of Israel and Judah would go through some terrible times. Many of them would be killed and others would be taken from their land. They would have to face the judgment and wrath of God for their choices. Even with all of this, God promises to restore their joy and comfort them. That same promise is available to us today.

Emotions are like thermostats. They tell you where your thoughts are, even those deep subconscious thoughts that you are not aware of. So, take your temperature. How do you rank on the joy scale? If you find that your joy index is a little low, we have great news for you. You can raise that index immediately. You have, within you, all you need to experience all of the joy you desire. You have the Holy Spirit.

That's right. The Holy Spirit produces joy among other things in your life. Remember Galatians 3:22-23? *"But the fruit of the Spirit is love, joy, peace, patience, kindness, goodness, faithfulness, gentleness and self-control. Against such things there is no law."* So where do we get this joy? The Holy Spirit produces joy in our lives. Along with joy, we can expect love, peace, patience, kindness, goodness, faithfulness, gentleness and self-control.

Today, spend some time meditating on God. Spend time communing with the Holy Spirit. You have total control over what you spend your thoughts on. Think on the goodness of God and all that He has done. Think about His majesty and how wonderful He is and think on His love for you. If you think on these things, you will experience the joy of the Lord.

Affirmations

I praise God for His Holy Spirit. When I walk in the Spirit, He produces joy in my life. I do not have to put up with sadness. I am so grateful for the promise that God will turn my mourning into joy and comfort me. In Jesus' name, Amen.

Day 12 - I Will Hearken to You

Scripture Lesson: Jeremiah 29:11-13

For I know the thoughts that I think toward you, saith the LORD, thoughts of peace, and not of evil, to give you an expected end. Then shall ye call upon me, and ye shall go and pray unto me, and I will hearken unto you. And ye shall seek me, and find me, when ye shall search for me with all your heart.

Meditation

God had a plan for Israel. His plan was to make them a great nation. However, the Israelites were not cooperating. They had forsaken God many times and were now paying the price. They were in captivity. However, God had not given up on them. Although things did not look good right now, God still had a plan. However, the Israelites would have to do their part.

Our promise today comes from a letter that God told Jeremiah to write the remaining elders of Jerusalem. He basically told them to get comfortable where they were. Although other prophets were saying that they would be delivered soon, God had warned them that they would be there for 70 years, and 70 years it was. It would not be a day sooner. So, they might as well get comfortable. God told them to build houses, find wives and plant gardens. They would be there awhile.

However, after the 70 years, God would bring them back. He had a plan, but they would have to cooperate. Why would they have to do anything if it was God's plan? God's plan does not supersede our free will. Look at our scripture for today, and see all the things that we are required to do. "Then shall you call upon me. You shall go and pray unto me. You shall seek me, and find me and search for me with all your heart." The promise of "I will hearken unto you" comes with all of these requirements. Not only must we diligently seek Him, we must find Him.

As born again Christians, our search for God has been made easy by the Holy Spirit. We do not have to travel to various locations or seek Him through strange means. The Bible tells us not only is the Holy Spirit in us, but Jesus and God are also in us. Now that we know where He is, we must call on Him and yield to His direction.

Affirmations

God has a plan for me. I will cooperate. God has thoughts of peace toward me. Those include completeness, health, tranquility, prosperity, and the absence of agitation or discord. I know where to find God because the Bible says He is in me. I am so grateful for the promise that God will hearken unto me. In Jesus' name, Amen.

Day 13 - I Will Set Him on High

Scripture Lesson: Psalm 91:14-16

> *Because he hath set his love upon me, therefore will I deliver him: I will set him on high, because he hath known my name. He shall call upon me, and I will answer him: I will be with him in trouble; I will deliver him, and honour him. With long life will I satisfy him, and shew him my salvation.*

Meditation

The 91st Psalm is considered a Psalm of Trust. It is a psalm that can be used in just about any situation. It's hard to read this passage and not feel a warm sensation inside. It is so comforting, and it always seems to make you feel better, no matter what is going on.

This psalm contains tremendous promises from the Lord. He promises to deliver us, set us on high, answer us, be with us in trouble, honor us, satisfy us with long life and show us His salvation. There's not too much that doesn't fall into this realm. What do we need to do in order to enjoy these promises? We need to set our love upon Him, know His name and call upon Him. This is not hard to do, because our God is an awesome God.

For the rest of our meditation, let's read the words of the entire 91st Psalm as recorded in the New Living Translation. See the images in your mind as you read the words. Hear the voice of God as you read the promises at the end. Our God is truly an awesome God.

> *Those who live in the shelter of the Most High will find rest in the shadow of the Almighty. This I declare about the Lord: He alone is my refuge, my place of safety; he is my God, and I trust him. For he will rescue you from every trap and protect you from deadly disease. He will cover you with his feathers. He will shelter you with his wings. His faithful promises are your armor and protection. Do not be afraid of the terrors of the night, nor the arrow that flies in the day. Do not dread the disease that stalks in darkness, nor the disaster that strikes at midday. Though a thousand fall at your side, though ten thousand are dying around you, these evils will not touch you. Just open your eyes, and see how the wicked are punished. If you make the Lord your refuge, if you make the Most High your shelter, no evil will conquer you; no plague will come near your home. For he will order his angels to protect you wherever you go. They will hold you up with their hands so you won't even hurt your foot on a stone. You will trample upon lions and cobras; you will crush fierce lions and serpents under your feet! The Lord says, "I will rescue those who love me. I will protect those who trust in my name. When they call on me, I will answer; I will be with them in trouble. I will rescue and honor them. I will reward them with a long life and give them my salvation."*

Affirmations

My God is awesome. I love Him and I call upon Him. I am so grateful for the promise that God will deliver me, set me on high, be with me in times of trouble, honor me, satisfy me with long life and show me His salvation. In Jesus' name, Amen.

Day 14 - I Will Restore to You the Years

Scripture Lesson: Joel 2:25

And I will restore to you the years that the locust hath eaten, the cankerworm, and the caterpillar, and the palmerworm, my great army which I sent among you.

Meditation

The 2nd chapter of Joel begins with a devastating prophecy concerning locust. Destruction was eminent, because Judah would not obey God. He warns them how terrible this plague would be. However, He also asked them to turn back to Him. He tells them that He is gracious and merciful, slow to anger, and of great kindness. He loves them and He wants their love in return.

As a loving God, He is a God of restoration. Throughout this chapter, God promises Judah restoration. This is where we find our promise for today. He promised restoration for the years that were eaten up by locust and cankerworm. By nature, when locusts attack crops, not only do they eat up the current harvest, but they also destroy the buds and seeds of future harvests. God promises not only to restore the harvest, but also to restore the years of future produce. What a wonderful God we serve!

This promise tells us about the nature of God. Not only will God restore the things that we have lost due to our own poor choices, He will also restore our dreams and the future of those dreams. Just turn to God. In true relationship and fellowship with Him, He will lead and guide you. He will restore lost opportunities and chances. It is never too late. He is a God of restoration.

Affirmations

God is a God of restoration. I know God loves me and I know that I love God. I am so grateful for the promise that God will restore unto me the years that have been eaten up by the locust of poor choices and bad decisions. In Jesus' name, Amen.

Day 15 - My Word Shall Not Return to Me Void

Scripture Lesson: Isaiah 55:10-11

For as the rain cometh down, and the snow from heaven, and returneth not thither, but watereth the earth, and maketh it bring forth and bud, that it may give seed to the sower, and bread to the eater: So shall my word be that goeth forth out of my mouth: it shall not return unto me void, but it shall accomplish that which I please, and it shall prosper in the thing whereto I sent it.

Meditation

God has faith in His words. He explains through Isaiah, the prophet, that His words are like rain on the earth. The purpose of rain and snow is to water the earth. That water makes the earth bring forth. The earth cannot decide that it does not want to produce. If you give it enough water and sunlight, something will grow, even if it is weeds.

God further explains that His words will not return to Him void. They can't. He has commanded them using the words "shall not". It is like God is speaking to His words. He tells them that they "shall not" return to Him void. He then instructs the words as to what they should do. His words are to accomplish what He pleases, and they are to prosper the thing He sends it to. God's words are powerful.

But guess what? He has given our words the same power. We are told in Mark 11:23 that our words are just as powerful. However, we must believe and not doubt. Jesus gives us a clue in Mark 11:22 that is often overlooked because of how it was translated in the King James Version. We typically read this passage to say "Have faith in God". However, more literal translations, such as the 1898 Young's Literal Translation reads, "Have faith of God". So we are told here that we must have the same kind of faith that God has. God says that His words will accomplish what He pleases. Jesus says that you shall have what you say. God says that His word shall not return to Him void. Jesus says that you must believe and not doubt that whatever you say shall come to past. God and Jesus are saying the same thing.

If you don't like what you have, stop saying what you are saying. Things do work out for you. You are successful. You do accomplish anything you put your mind to. You are just like your Father. You have what you say.

Affirmations

I am just like my Heavenly Father. His word prosper the things it is sent to and so do mine. His word accomplishes what He pleases and so do mine. I am so grateful for the promise that God's Word does not return to Him void. Neither does mine. In Jesus' name, Amen.

Day 16 - I Will Not Fail Thee

Scripture Lesson: Joshua 1:5
There shall not any man be able to stand before thee all the days of thy life: as I was with Moses, so I will be with thee: I will not fail thee, nor forsake thee.

Meditation

Joshua had a tremendous task ahead of him. His mentor and teacher, Moses, was dead and now he was expected to finish the work that God started with Moses. There were so many challenges to overcome. He had a lot of people to lead who had a history of not having the greatest respect for leadership and authority. They were not familiar with this new territory. There was no map that they could refer to; they just had to trust God to lead them. And then, of course, there were the people that still lived in the land. They would have to fight for this land. It was not like they could just walk up to someone's house and say, "Hi, we are the children of Israel and God has given us your land." They would have to fight.

Joshua needed a word of encouragement to complete this task. That word would come directly from God. This is where we find our promise for today. God promises Joshua that He would not fail or forsake him. He also tells him that He would be with him just has He had been with Moses. That is a huge promise because God and Moses had a strong relationship. To some it was unbelievable. God and Moses would talk for hours at a time. God even showed Himself, as much as He could, to Moses. The Bible claims that Moses was considered a friend of God. Now, God was telling Joshua that He would be with Him just like He was with Moses. What an awesome thought.

For the Christian, this awesome thought is nothing compared with the relationship we now have with God. God is with us and in us. He will not fail us and He will not leave us. As we face challenges that seem impossible to overcome, realize that the entire power of the universe resides in you, because God is in you. We cannot fail, because God will not fail us. Therefore, we must change how we view situations in our lives. When things do not happen as we would like, we must learn from those situations and allow that knowledge to propel us to the next level. Remember, God is with us.

Affirmations

I am a friend of God. No matter what challenges I face, God is with me. I am never alone. I am gratefully rejoicing for the promise that God will never fail me or forsake me. In Jesus' name, Amen.

Day 17 - I Will Magnify You

Scripture Lesson: Joshua 3:7

> *And the LORD said unto Joshua, This day will I begin to magnify thee in the sight of all Israel, that they may know that, as I was with Moses, so I will be with thee.*

Meditation

As we discussed yesterday, Joshua had a challenging task to complete. He had to make sure that the children of Israel acquired the land that God had promised them. There were battles to fight as well as land to oversee. He had to insure that the right tribe got the right land and that everything was done as God had instructed through Moses. This would require a lot of hard, diligent work on Joshua's part. That was fine because that was something that Joshua could control. It would also require that Joshua had the respect of his people as well as the nations he was going up against. This was something that Joshua could not control. He would need God's help.

God was ready to help. In our promise today, God tells Joshua that He would begin to magnify him in the sight of all Israel so that everyone would know that God was with him, just like He was with Moses. God would magnify Joshua. We are accustomed to reading the Bible's instructions for man to magnify God, but here God is saying that He would magnify man. What a phenomenal thought.

Many times we find ourselves in a similar situation as Joshua. We are facing tasks that are challenging. Although we have been called by God to complete the challenge, we may feel that we are always trying to prove ourselves to others. If we have been called to complete a task that was started by someone it, it can be difficult to gain the trust and respect of the people, especially if the previous person was strong and well liked. Often, we spend too much time trying to prove ourselves. Responding to statements such as "Our previous leader didn't do it like this" or "We have always done it this way" can be frustrating and counterproductive.

Praise God that you do not have to face this alone. We often say that God never calls you to an assignment that He has not equipped you to do. He will help you. Not only are you anointed with the power to complete the task, He will magnify in the eyes of the people. The power of God in you will cause people to respect and admire you. However, with such power and charisma comes responsibility. Make sure that you treat people in a way that deserves their respect.

Affirmation

I am equipped to complete any task that God assigns me to. I can face the challenge and gain the respect of people because I show God's love to everyone I meet. I am gratefully rejoicing for the promise that God will magnify me. In Jesus Name, Amen.

Day 18 - I Will Teach Thee to Profit

Scripture Lesson: Isaiah 48:17
> *Thus saith the LORD, thy Redeemer, the Holy One of Israel; I am the LORD thy God which teacheth thee to profit, which leadeth thee by the way that thou shouldest go.*

Meditation

You can tell a lot about a person by their conversation. A person's conversation can give you insight about their personality. Some people are very analytical so they like to analyze the events of the day. Some people like to look at situations through the eyes of humor. So they will make jokes about current events and see the lighter side of things. Some people are paranoid and suspicious so they question everything. You also get an idea of a person's core values by their conversation.

In the 48th chapter of Isaiah, you get to see some of the personality of God through His conversation. You can see that God is a caring and compassionate God. He tells them that He warned them about the terrible things that would happen to Israel long time ago, but they would not listen. You can see that God is confident. He tells them that He alone is God. He is Alpha and Omega. You can also tell that one of God's core values is for His people to prosper.

It is in this conversation that we find our promise for today. He tells Israel that He is the God that teaches and directs. He teaches them how to profit and leads them in the way they should go. God tells them if they had only listened to Him and followed His commandment, they would have had peace flowing like a river. God wanted them to live a fulfilling, success life that was profitable. He did not want them owing anyone. He would teach them to profit.

What an awesome promise! For a business to make a profit, it must make more money than it spends. Every company in business must make more than they spend in order to stay open. Businesses spend millions of dollars on books, programs and consultants every year trying to figure out how to do this. Yet we hear God promising Israel that He will teach them to profit. That promise is available to us today. But we must not be afraid to step out on the things that God tells us to do.

So don't be afraid of those great, money making ideas that are inspired by God. Notice, it did not say that He was the God that teaches us just how to get by, but the God that teaches us how to profit. God has not changed. He is still the best business consultant there is. His book, the Bible, has been on the best sellers' list for as long as there has been one.

Affirmations

God wants me to be successful. He has promised to lead and guide me. I will follow His instructions and seek Him when I am confused. I am gratefully rejoicing for the promise that God will teach me to profit. In Jesus' name, Amen.

Day 19 - I Sanctified Thee

Scripture Lesson: Jeremiah 1:4-5
Then the word of the LORD came unto me, saying, Before I formed thee in the belly I knew thee; and before thou camest forth out of the womb I sanctified thee, and I ordained thee a prophet unto the nations.

Meditation

There are so many great nuggets from our scripture today. Our promise for today is really more of a fact, than a promise. God tells Jeremiah that before he was formed, God knew him. How can God know us before conception? Because we are not flesh and blood; we are spirit. We are spirit, we have a soul and we live in a body. However, before our soul, which includes our minds and emotions, and before our physical bodies began to form, we were spirit. And we were known by God.

He then tells Jeremiah that He sanctified him before he was born. The word sanctified means to set apart as holy. Before Jeremiah was even born, God set him aside as holy. He goes on to say that He ordained Jeremiah to be a prophet to the nations.

Just as with Jeremiah, God knew each of us before we were ever physically conceived. We were spirit, and we were with Him. God has also set us aside and has a plan for us. Just as God told Jeremiah in chapter 29:11, God knows the thoughts that He has towards us. We may not all be called to be prophets to the nations, but we are called to spread His word.

In the next few verses, Jeremiah tells God that he cannot do this task, because he is only a child, as if God did not know his age. God tells Jeremiah that He does not want to hear his excuses. Before He comforts Jeremiah, He gets him straight. He tells Jeremiah that you are going to do whatever I tell you to do. Then He comforts him by telling him not to be afraid of the faces of his enemies because God would deliver him.

God has sanctified and set us apart also. Not because of the church we belong to or by any act of our own. He sanctified us because He has a work for us to do. You are not here by accident. You were not a mistake. You may not have been planned by your parents, but you part of the infinite plan of God. You are here for a reason.

Affirmations

I am here for a reason. God knew me before I was conceived. I am not a mistake. I am part of God's infinite plan. I am gratefully rejoicing for the fact that God has sanctified me. In Jesus' name, Amen.

Day 20 - I Will Answer Thee

Scripture Lesson: Jeremiah 33:3

Call unto me, and I will answer thee, and show thee great and mighty things, which thou knowest not.

Meditation

Sometimes the simplest things can seem so hard, especially when we look for it to be complicated. Take communication for instance. Although talking is easy, communication takes a little more work. Anyone can say words. However, to be an artful communicator, you must make sure that your words relay the message that you intended to the right person and that they understood your message. Even though this may take a little more effort on your part, it does not have to be hard.

Communication with God is not as hard as some make it out to be. Some people believe that you have to be at a certain place, at a certain time, in order to hear from God. Others say that you have to act a certain way in order for God to talk to you. And then there are others that say God will not talk to you unless you are like them.

God gives very simple instructions on how to reach Him. You don't have to have a special number, sit or lay a special way, or go to a special place. He tells us to just call on Him. That's it. Just call on Him. He promises that if we call on Him, He will answer us. Not only will He answer us, but He will show us great and mighty things that we don't know about.

Have you ever asked God about something and then at some point received an answer that you knew was from God? Perhaps the answer revealed knowledge that you just didn't know on your own. You figured out something that you knew you could not have figured out if it had not been for what we call "divine intervention". You may call it instinct or the universe talking. It is God talking. He may drop something directly into your spirit, or He may lead someone to give you the answer. You may come across the answer in a book or see a billboard on the expressway. Either way, God is communicating with you. Just make sure that you take the time to listen. When we do all the talking in prayer, we can't hear the answers that are being revealed.

So, before you call your good girl friend or your buddy, call on God. He's not too busy. He'll answer. He's waiting on your call.

Affirmations

I have great communication with God. He talks to me and I listen. He is never too busy to take my call. I am so grateful for the promise that God will answer me. In Jesus' name, Amen.

Day 21 - The Just Shall Live By His Faith

Scripture Lesson: Habakkuk 2:2-4

And the LORD answered me, and said, Write the vision, and make it plain upon tables, that he may run that readeth it. For the vision is yet for an appointed time, but at the end it shall speak, and not lie: though it tarry, wait for it; because it will surely come, it will not tarry. Behold, his soul which is lifted up is not upright in him: but the just shall live by his faith.

Meditation

Very little is known about Habakkuk except that he was a prophet and author of the book which bears his name. The book of Habakkuk is a snap shot of a conversation between God and Habakkuk. Habakkuk asked God a question, got an answer that he did not like, asked God a follow up question, received additional information, and then told God thank you in a prayer and a song.

Habakkuk wanted to know how long there would be corruption in Judah. They had laws, but they were not enforced. As a result, people were getting away with everything. God answers Habakkuk and tells him don't worry. He is about to destroy Judah with the Chaldeans.

That was like taking a machine gun to kill a fly. That was not the answer that Habakkuk was looking for. He just wanted his people to treat each other fairly. Why would God use a nation that was more sinful than Judah to correct her? And why them? They were the most treacherous, evil people he knew. And furthermore, they did not even believe in God. They were idol worshippers. They would beat God's people, and then they would worship their idols. In Habakkuk's mind, God needed to think this through.

God's response to Habakkuk's concerns is where we find our promise for today. The Lord was going to use the Chaldeans to chastise Judah, but He would also destroy the Chaldeans because of their evil doings. No one was getting away with anything. God told Habakkuk to write it down; even though the vision may not come right away, just wait on it. In the end, it would happen just as God said it would. The just shall live by his faith.

It seems as if God was telling Habakkuk not to worry so much about the injustices around him, but to remember his faith. These words are good for us also. We sometimes get caught up in why the ungodly prosper while we struggle. We must take our focus off of them and focus on God. We live by our faith. Notice, this verse does not say that the just shall live by faith, it says that the just shall live by "his" faith. You cannot live by other people's faith. You must live by your faith.

What do you believe? Whatever it is, that is what you will experience. If you believe that God is limited, then you will experience the limits of God. If you believe that God is unlimited, you will experience the fullness of God. As Jesus said, "According to "your" faith, be it unto you".

Affirmations

I am the righteousness of God, and I live by my faith. I believe in the power of God, and I see that power at work in my life every day. I am so grateful for the promise that I can live by my faith. In Jesus' name, Amen.

Day 22 - I Will Give Thee Riches and Wealth

Scripture Lesson: 2 Chronicles 1:12

Wisdom and knowledge is granted unto thee; and I will give thee riches, and wealth, and honour, such as none of the kings have had that have been before thee, neither shall there any after thee have the like.

Meditation

It is often interesting to hear how couples met. Can you imagine Solomon answering the question, "So how did your parents meet?" In order to be truthful, he would have to say that his father first saw his mother taking a bath on a roof top. He sent for her, and that was all she wrote. He would have to include the fact that she was married to another man at the time. Then, of course, he would have to add that his father had his mother's husband killed because he had gotten her pregnant. Then for good measure, he could throw in the fact that the child was killed by God because of what happened. Not a typical, romantic story that you would want to share with your friends. However, it was Solomon's story.

With all of this family drama, God still chose Solomon to lead Israel. It was a big job. But to help him out, God paid a visit to Solomon in a dream and told him to ask for whatever he wanted. Instead of wealth and riches or political strength, Solomon asked for wisdom and knowledge so that he could do a good job.

God's response to Solomon is where we find our scripture for today. Although this was a promise directly to Solomon and not a blanket promise to everyone, it does reveal the heart and nature of God. God was so impressed with his answer that He told him that He would give him wisdom and knowledge plus all of the stuff he didn't ask for, like wealth, riches and honor. What does this reveal about God?

It appears that God did not have a problem with Solomon being wealthy. He did not have a problem with Solomon being honored among men. He did not have a problem with Solomon being very successful. God didn't appear to have a problem with the fact that He chose Solomon to be king and that Solomon would not be perfect. In fact, the riches and wealth were going to attract Solomon to some things that would eventually turn Solomon's heart away from God. God freely gave those things to Solomon, knowing that Solomon would make mistakes, and even with all of his wisdom, he would make some wrong choices.

The same can be said about us. With all of the anointing that we have, we still make wrong choices. There are consequences for those choices, but God never turns His back on us. Neither does His nature change towards us. The scripture tells us that God gives richly all things to enjoy and that He takes pleasure in the prosperity of His servants.

Affirmations

God gives me richly all things to enjoy. God takes pleasure in the prosperity of his servants. Not only am I a servant of God but I am a child of God. I ask God for more wisdom and knowledge so that I can make better choices. I am so grateful for scriptures that reveal God's heart. I, too, can have wealth, riches and honor. In Jesus' name, Amen.

Day 23 - You Shall Be a Peculiar Treasure Unto Me

Scripture Lesson: Exodus 19:5-6

Now therefore, if ye will obey my voice indeed, and keep my covenant, then ye shall be a peculiar treasure unto me above all people: for all the earth is mine: And ye shall be unto me a kingdom of priests, and an holy nation. These are the words which thou shalt speak unto the children of Israel.

Meditation

The children of Israel were precious to God. They were His chosen people. He did not choose them because they were better than other people. He chose them because... He chose them. He does not give us reason. All we know is that they were chosen.

It appears that God wanted a people that He could have intimate relationship with. He wanted a people that appreciated Him for who He was, God Almighty. He wanted them to know His strength and respect it. He would do mighty things for them, but in return He wanted them to obey His voice. If they did, they would be a peculiar treasure to Him, a kingdom of priest and a holy, consecrated nation.

Not only is this promise for us today as believers, but it is repeated, in 1 Peter 2:9. "*But ye are a chosen generation, a royal priesthood, an holy nation, a peculiar people; that ye should shew forth the praises of him who hath called you out of darkness into his marvelous light.*"

We are a treasure to God. Imagine that, a treasure to the Almighty God. We must show forth His praise and recognize that He called us out of darkness into His marvelous light. We are no longer in the darkness of sin. We can now walk according to the spirit.

Are you acting like a treasure to God? Do you appreciate not only what He has done for you but who He is to you? If so, show forth His praise and let others know about the goodness of God.

Affirmations

I am precious to God. I am important to God. I am chosen, royal, holy and peculiar. I will recognize my importance to Him by showing forth His praise. I am so grateful for the promise that I am a peculiar treasure to God. In Jesus' name, Amen.

Day 24 - I Will Not Leave Thee

Scripture Lesson: Genesis 28:15

And, behold, I am with thee, and will keep thee in all places whither thou goest, and will bring thee again into this land; for I will not leave thee, until I have done that which I have spoken to thee of.

Meditation

Jacob found himself in a very interesting place. Upon the coaching of his mother, he had stolen his brother's blessing. His brother had vowed to kill him so Jacob was on the run. He was headed to his uncle's home in the hopes of finding a wife and giving his brother some time to cool off. But would his brother ever "cool off"? Esau was known for being hot headed. Jacob had really done it this time. Esau was determined to get him, and there was no one who could save him.

As Jacob travels to his uncle's, he stopped along the way to sleep. Apparently sleeping outside, he takes stones to make a pillow. That night he dreams of a ladder that reaches heaven with angels of God ascending and descending. He then sees God at the top of the ladder. It is here that we find our promise for today.

God confirms his covenant with Jacob, as He did with Abraham and Isaac. He promises to multiply his seed as the dust on the earth and to give to him the land he promised his father and grandfather. God promises to be with Jacob and to keep him wherever he goes. He also assures him that He will bring him back to this land and that He will not leave Jacob until He had done what He has promised.

What does this reveal about the nature of God? The first thing it shows us is God's faithfulness to those He has chosen. Jacob was a trickster. Jacob had not only stolen Esau's blessing but had tricked him out of his birthright. However, he was now chosen by God and God was going to stand by him. We also see that God does not leave work undone. Although Jacob would be gone for at least 14 years, God promised to bring him back on the land and not leave him.

This is also true of God in the life of the believer. Jesus assures us in Matthew 28:20 that He will be with us until the end of the world. No matter what we are going through or what we face, God is always with us. He will never leave us or forsake us. We can depend on that.

Affirmations

God is with me. He will keep me wherever I go. He will bring me into my land of promise. I am so grateful for the promise that God will not leave me. In Jesus' name, Amen.

Day 25 - I Will Make the Crooked Places Straight

Scripture Lesson: Isaiah 45:1-3

Thus saith the LORD to his anointed, to Cyrus, whose right hand I have holden, to subdue nations before him; and I will loose the loins of kings, to open before him the two leaved gates; and the gates shall not be shut; I will go before thee, and make the crooked places straight: I will break in pieces the gates of brass, and cut in sunder the bars of iron: And I will give thee the treasures of darkness, and hidden riches of secret places, that thou mayest know that I, the LORD, which call thee by thy name, am the God of Israel.

Meditation

The power of the prophetic word is often not understood until its fulfillment. God used Isaiah in such an awesome way that many theologians cannot believe that Isaiah wrote the entire book that bears his name. They believe that the second part of the book of Isaiah had to be written by someone else because there is no way Isaiah could have prophesied, by name, the king that God would use to rebuild the temple, 150 years before it happened. However, God knows who He will use.

God promises Cyrus that He will give him treasures and riches that are hidden. He will do this so that Cyrus will know that the Lord is the God of Israel. He also promises to make the crooked places straight and break in pieces the gates of brass and cut in sunder the bars of iron. Forget about opening doors. God is promising here to break down the doors. What a mighty God we serve!

There is nothing too hard for God. There is nothing that is outside of God's reach. God can speak of events 150 years before they happen. Cyrus would be born for a purpose.

We were also born for a purpose. God is also with us. He will go before us. God will break into pieces the gates that hold us back from our destiny. God will also give us treasures and hidden riches so that we will know that He is God. And God will make our crooked places straight.

Affirmations

God is with me. There are no doors that can hinder me from my destiny. God will lead and guide me on my path. I am so grateful for the promise that God will make my crooked places straight. In Jesus' name, Amen.

Day 26 - I Will Cause Breath to Enter You

Scripture Lesson: Ezekiel 37:5

Thus saith the Lord GOD unto these bones; Behold, I will cause breath to enter into you, and ye shall live:

Meditation

One of the first stories you probably heard from the book of Ezekiel was about the valley of dry bones. According to Ezekiel, God took him to a valley of dry bones where he was to prophesy to the bones and God would put muscle and skin on them. God told Ezekiel that he would also breathe into the bones and bring life to them. From this, these bones, which represented the nation of Israel, would know that the Lord was God.

We have also heard exegesis on what these dry bones represent in our lives today. Some believe these bones represent our dreams and hopes that have somehow become deferred. Some believe that these dry bones represent the spirituality of man without God. Whatever these bones represent, they experienced total restoration through God.

One of the interesting things in this chapter is how God used Ezekiel to be part of the solution. Although God could have addressed these bones without Ezekiel, there appears to be dominion principles represented here that need to be examined more closely.

The first thing God does is show Ezekiel the problem. Without acknowledging there is a problem, the solution will not be sought after. He then asks Ezekiel if he thinks these bones can live. Although Ezekiel doesn't know the answer, he does not give God a negative response. He defers to God and tells him that only He knows. However, the question that God asks Ezekiel starts him thinking about the solution.

God then instructs Ezekiel to prophesy to the bones. Ezekiel must speak to the bones and tell them how God is going to restore them. But that's not all. Once the muscle and skin was on the bones, the bones were not alive. Ezekiel had to prophesy to the wind and tell it to breath into the bones. It was only then that life came into the bones and they became a mighty army.

Do you have a few dry bones around that need restoration? Are you looking for a prophetic word from the Lord that would speak life into your dry situation? You already have it, the Word of God. You don't have to wait for a prophet to stand you up and speak a word of hope to your situation. You can prophesy to your dry bones. Speak to the resources that you need in order to accomplish the dreams and goals that you have. Speak life into your situation, whether it is health, finances, relationships, or peace of mind. You have the authority and ability to do it. You have the Spirit of God living on the inside of you.

Affirmations

I have the Spirit of God living on the inside of me. I can speak the Word of God to my dry bones and see miraculous changes. I am so grateful for the promise that God will cause breath to enter my dry bones, and they will live. In Jesus' name, Amen.

Day 27 - I Shall Put My Spirit In You

Scripture Lesson: Ezekiel 37:14
And shall put my spirit in you, and ye shall live, and I shall place you in your own land: then shall ye know that I the LORD have spoken it, and performed it, saith the LORD.

Meditation

We continue to look at the story of Ezekiel and the valley of dry bones. As we saw in the previous lesson, Ezekiel was instructed to prophesy to a valley of dry bones which represented the nation of Israel. God promised to restore Israel and make the nation a mighty army. We also looked at how the dry bones could represent things of today such as broken dreams or bad situations. We established that we, just as Ezekiel did, could prophesy to our situations and see the miracle of God's restoration.

Today's promise is found in that same story. God tells Israel that He will put His spirit in them, and they shall live. This has been fulfilled today through the anointing of the Holy Spirit. Although we know this intellectually, many times we don't understand the importance of it. Just think about it. God's has put His spirit in you. The almighty power of the universe lives in you. Not only does the earth show forth God's glory, you show forth His glory.

That power makes it possible for you to live. Not just have breath, but to live, to have an abundant life. Everything you need is within you because God is within you. He leads and guides you. He protects you. He supplies your needs. All you have to do is believe.

It's easy to believe when everything is going well. However, it is when things are difficult that believing becomes challenging. Don't despair. You are well able to meet this challenge. Determine that you will obey God's Word. Speak to your circumstances. Prophesy words of hope to your situation. Then trust God. Know that God has spoken it and performed it.

Affirmations

God's Spirit lives inside of me. I am His child. I will obey His Word. I will prophesy hope to my situation and trust God to restore. I am so grateful for the promise that God has put His spirit in me so that I can live. In Jesus' name, Amen.

Day 28 - I Am For You

Scripture Lesson: Ezekiel 36:9

For, behold, I am for you, and I will turn unto you, and ye shall be tilled and sown:

Meditation

As we have discussed before, Israel was in a state of confusion. They had turned from God. As a result, they would experience the wrath of God. They would be in captivity, driven from their land. This was a direct result of their disobedience.

Even when God was angry with Israel, He still spoke words of hope and restoration. Israel would be punished for turning from God and turning to idols. However, God would not let them be totally destroyed. He would restore them. It is here that we find our promise for today.

God told Israel that He was for them. If God be for you, who can be against you? This does not mean no one will be against you. It compares the power of God being for you against the powerlessness of anyone else that would be against you.

Meditate on our scripture, "I am for you". Hear God say this to your spirit. He is for you. He is not just in you, but He is for you. He is cheering for you. He is by your side. He wants you to be successful. He loves you.

Notice that He also tells Israel that He would turn to them and that they would be tilled and sown. This speaks of being taken care of. He would see to them and make sure that they had everything that they needed to grow. What an awesome God!

As Christians, God has also promised to tend to us in a similar fashion. We remember in John chapter 15 where Jesus explains the true vine. Jesus tells us that God will be the gardener. He will tend and care for us. But He will also prune us so that we are fruitful. Even though pruning is not always pleasant, it is necessary for our growth. We will be better for it.

So remember, God is for you. No situation that you are facing is designed to overtake or conquer you. You are more than a conqueror, because God is for you.

Affirmations

God is on my side. He cares about me and my situation. I will trust Him and know that He will take care of me. I am so grateful for the promise that God is for me. In Jesus' name, Amen.

Day 29 - I Will Pour My Spirit Upon All Flesh

Scripture Lesson: Joel 2:28

> *And it shall come to pass afterward, that I will pour out my spirit upon all flesh; and your sons and your daughters shall prophesy, your old men shall dream dreams, your young men shall see visions.*

Meditation

We often hear that everyone is talented and gifted in some area. But if you have not yet discovered your area, it can be very frustrating. You may seem to be surrounded by people that know what they want out of life, and they seem to be equipped to get it. It may not be the same for you. You may not have discovered your passion. This can make you feel that you are not as special, talented or gifted as others. This is not the case.

In the Old Testament, there were people that were, for lack of better words, more special than others. This "special" designation came from God Himself. He would allow His Spirit to interact with only a special group of people. You had to be a king, priest or a prophet to be able to interact with the Spirit of God on a regular basis. If you were not lucky enough to be part of one of these groups, you had to get with someone from one of these groups to hear from God. It seemed as if God didn't just talk to anybody. You had to be special. There was no "open door" policy in heaven.

In the New Testament, all of that changed. The sacrifice that Jesus made on the cross literally opened up heaven. Along with the wonderful gift of salvation, we received the gift of the Holy Spirit. As God promised in Joel, He poured His Spirit upon all flesh. You do not have to be born into a privileged family or have a special occupation to receive this gift. You don't have to consult a king, priest, pastor or prophet to talk to God. He is right there with you right now!

No one in the Body of Christ is more special than someone else. You may be extremely talented and gifted, or you may not. You may live what others judge to be a "sanctified life", or you may be a real cut up. In any case, you are special and important to God. You can access Him at any time. Through the Holy Spirit, there is an open door policy in heaven. You can go boldly before the throne of grace at any time and commune with God. Isn't it nice to be special!

Affirmations

Father, I thank you for the Holy Spirit. I will no longer entertain thoughts of worthlessness or poor self-esteem. It is so good to know that I am so special to You. I can come to You at any time. I am so grateful that You have poured your Spirit out upon me. In Jesus' name, Amen.

Day 30 - I Create New Heavens and a New Earth

Scripture Lesson: **Isaiah 65:17**

For, behold, I create new heavens and a new earth: and the former shall not be remembered, nor come into mind.

Meditation

There is something exciting about getting something new. Whether it is something small like a new tube of lipstick, a sweater or a new toy, or something larger like a new car or a new house, getting something new brings on an exuberating feeling. Getting something new often triggers a feeling of "new beginnings" or hope. We may even make a decision to do better in a certain area because of receiving something new.   For instance, we may decide that we will keep this new car cleaner than we did the old car. Getting something new can trigger a change in attitude and mindset.

Our promise today focuses on new items that are huge. It is not about new clothes, new gadgets, new cars or new houses. It is about a whole new world, complete with new heavens (notice that this is plural) and a new earth. This new world comes with a whole new operating system.   There is no crying in this new world.   All of the struggles that we have become accustomed to in this world are erased in this new world. There is no premature death in this new world.   People will enjoy the "work of their hands" and the accomplishments that they have made. As you read further in the passage, even the animal kingdom will operate under a new system, such that wolves and lambs will eat together.

Both the Apostles, Peter and John, saw this prophetically. Peter describes in 2 Peter 3:10-13 the passing away of the old heavens and earth. John describes seeing a new heaven and earth in Revelation 21:1. In this new earth, sometimes referred to as "New Jerusalem", everything is new; new streets, new gates, and even a new way to relate to God. We are told in Revelation 21 that God, Himself, will dwell in the city with His people. He will be such a light that even the sun and moon are relieved of their duties. Now that's a new world!

Affirmations

New things are coming into my life. I have a renewed sense of hope. I look forward to the new heavens and new earth that God has created. I am so grateful for the new outlook on life. I praise God that He is faithful. In Jesus' name, Amen.

Day 31 - I Am the Lord That Maketh All Things

Scripture Lesson: Isaiah 44:24

Thus saith the LORD, thy redeemer, and he that formed thee from the womb, I am the LORD that maketh all things; that stretcheth forth the heavens alone; that spreadeth abroad the earth by myself;

Meditation

There is nothing more frustrating than depending on a promise that is later broken. Many times people have good intentions and they try their very best to fulfill the promises they make but they are unable to. They really meant to call but ran out of time. They have every intention of coming but the car broke down. They really meant to do it but something beyond their control happened, and as a result, they were unable to keep their promise. When this happens, we understand. We, too, have been in this position where we intended to do something, but for whatever reason, we were unable to fulfill the promise.

What about when you are deceived? Sometimes people make promises that not only do they have no intention of keeping; they have no authority to make. A salesman can promise to lower your payments, but if he does not have the authority from the manager or owner, it won't get done. Sure, I can promise to sell you a mansion for a $1, but if I don't own the mansion or have authority to sell the mansion, I would not advise you to start packing. I would have made you an empty promise.

God does not make empty promises. His promises are not empty because He has authority to act on any promise He makes. As He clearly states in today's promise, He makes all things. He can make the promise because He owns the stuff. As He states, He is our redeemer. He formed us in our mother's womb. He made the heavens and the earth by Himself. Because He owns it all, He can declare a promise and it be fulfilled.

As we mentioned before, many theologians today have major problems with the idea that Isaiah authored chapters 40 through 66 of the book that bears his name because of the prophetic nature of the these chapters. How could Isaiah know the specific name of the king that God would use 150 years before? Easy. Just as an author can tell you how their book will end before they have actually written the words on paper, God can tell Isaiah the specifics of these incidents. God is the author. As stated in Isaiah 44:24-28, it is He (God) that can confirm the word of His servant and perform the counsel of His messengers.

In this volume, we have looked at some of the most precious promises of God. Some that many may believe are too good to be true. Can God really fulfill these promises concerning life here on earth and eternal life to follow? He surely can. He is the maker of life. He owns life. He designed life. He has the authority and the power to fulfill every promise made.

Affirmations

The God I serve is all powerful. He is able and has the authority to keep any and every promise that He makes. He is the maker of all things. I am gratefully for God's Word. In Jesus' name, Amen.

Notes

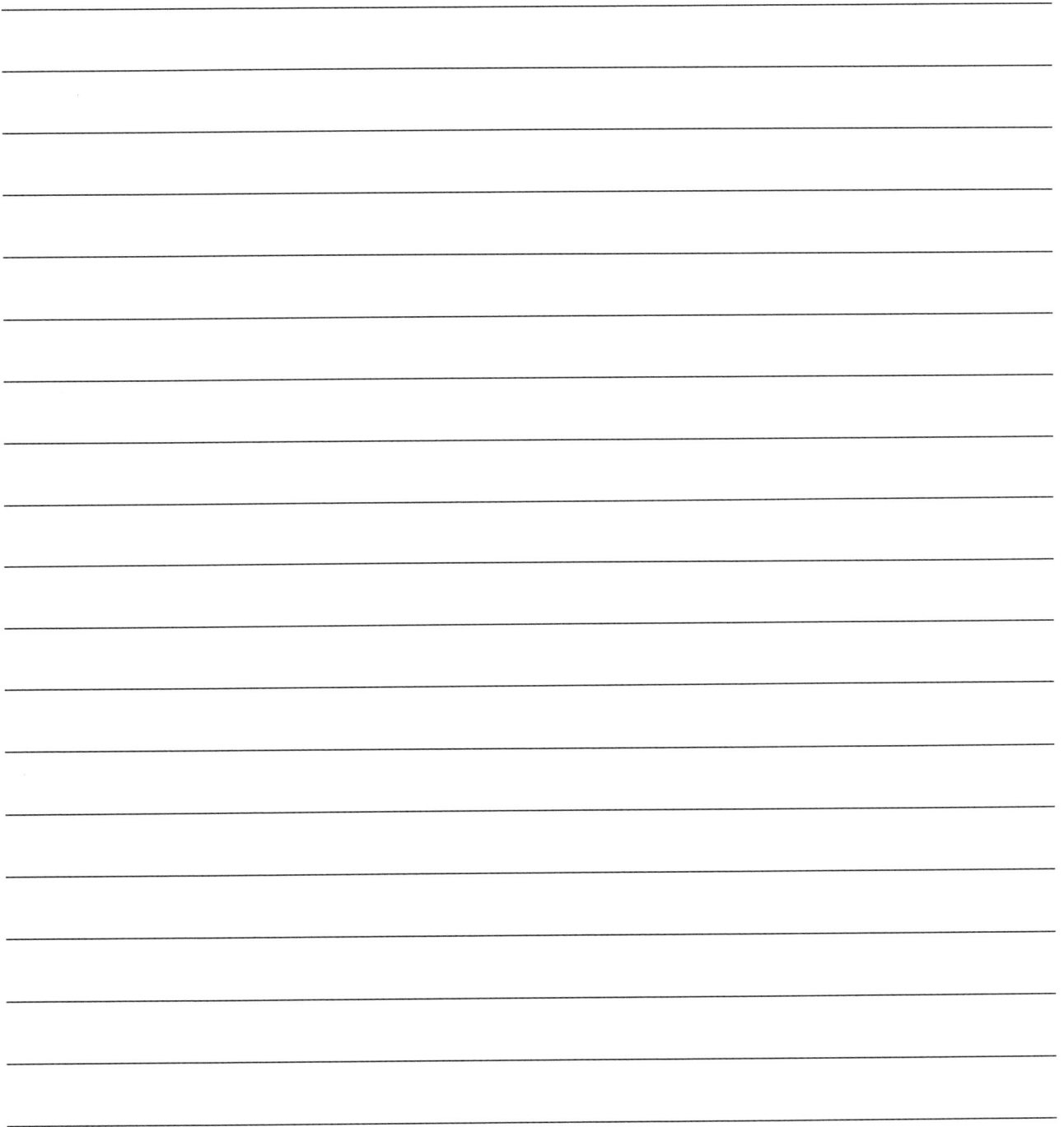

Other Books by Vanessa Collins

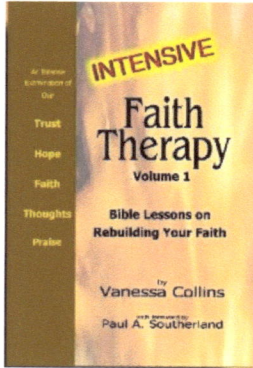

Intensive Faith Therapy
The Promises of Jesus

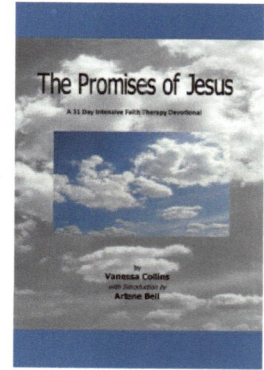

Looking for other materials to strengthen your faith?

Log on to www.IntensiveFaithTherapy.com

You can contact Vanessa Collins at Vanessa@intensivefaiththerapy.com or
Vancollins@aol.com

Look for us on Facebook
http://www.facebook.com/pages/Intensive-Faith-Therapy/111246621864

Follow us on Twitter
http://twitter.com/intensivefaith

Join our live class
http://pasenterprise.tv/IFT.html

www.ingramcontent.com/pod-product-compliance
Lightning Source LLC
Chambersburg PA
CBHW060812090426

42737CB00002B/38